Growing in the Gospel

The Psalms Project Volume Ten

Discovering the Spiritual World through the Psalms – Psalm 91-100

Michael Harvey Koplitz

TABLE OF CONTENTS

The goal of this project:

This research project will examine the 150 psalms for the spiritual awareness each Psalm offers. Each Psalm will be examined by its language and the commentary of the Sages. The spiritual awareness analysis will be done in alignment with Ari's definition of the Tree of life, the Book of Creation, and the Zohar. Each verse of the Psalm will be rewritten using the intent of the language and spiritual commentary to convey its spiritual lesson.

The main resources:

The Zohar

The Book of Creation

Ari's writing on the Tree of Life and the Ten Sefirot

The Theological Wordbook of the Old Testament

Samson Hirsch's commentary on the Psalms

Tehillim – Psalms – A new translation with a commentary anthologized from the Talmudic and rabbinic sources

Accordance Bible Software

Psalm 91

New American Standard 1995	Hebrew
Psa. 91:1 He who dwells in the [a]shelter of the Most High Will abide in the [b]shadow of the Almighty. 2 I will say to the LORD, "My [a]refuge and my [b]fortress, My God, in whom I [c]trust!" 3 For it is He who delivers you from the [a]snare of the trapper And from the deadly [b]pestilence. 4 He will [a]cover you with His pinions, And [b]under His wings you may seek refuge; His [c]faithfulness is a [d]shield and bulwark. **Psa. 91:5** You [a]will not be afraid of the [b]terror by night, Or of the [c]arrow that flies by day; 6 Of the [a]pestilence that [1]stalks in darkness, Or of the [b]destruction that lays waste at noon. 7 A thousand may fall at your side And ten thousand at your right hand, *But* [a]it shall not approach you. 8 You will only look on with your eyes And [a]see the recompense of the wicked. 9 [1]For you have made the LORD, [a]my refuge,	יֹשֵׁב בְּסֵתֶר עֶלְיֹון בְּצֵל שַׁדַּי **Psa. 91:1** יִתְלֹונָן : 2 אֹמַר לַיהוָה מַחְסִי וּמְצוּדָתִי אֱלֹהַי אֶבְטַח־בֹּו : 3 כִּי הוּא יַצִּילְךָ מִפַּח יָקוּשׁ מִדֶּבֶר הַוֹּות : 4 בְּאֶבְרָתֹו יָסֶךְ לָךְ וְתַחַת־ כְּנָפָיו תֶּחְסֶה צִנָּה וְסֹחֵרָה אֲמִתֹּו : 5 לֹא־תִירָא מִפַּחַד לָיְלָה מֵחֵץ יָעוּף יֹומָם : 6 מִדֶּבֶר בָּאֹפֶל יַהֲלֹךְ מִקֶּטֶב יָשׁוּד צָהֳרָיִם : 7 יִפֹּל מִצִּדְּךָ אֶלֶף וּרְבָבָה מִימִינֶךָ אֵלֶיךָ לֹא יִגָּשׁ : 8 רַק בְּעֵינֶיךָ תַבִּיט וְשִׁלֻּמַת רְשָׁעִים תִּרְאֶה : 9 כִּי־אַתָּה יְהוָה מַחְסִי עֶלְיֹון שַׂמְתָּ מְעֹונֶךָ : 10 לֹא־תְאֻנֶּה אֵלֶיךָ רָעָה וְנֶגַע לֹא־יִקְרַב בְּאָהֳלֶךָ : 11 כִּי מַלְאָכָיו יְצַוֶּה־לָּךְ לִשְׁמָרְךָ בְּכָל־דְּרָכֶיךָ : 12 עַל־ כַּפַּיִם יִשָּׂאוּנְךָ פֶּן־תִּגֹּף בָּאֶבֶן רַגְלֶךָ : 13 עַל־שַׁחַל וָפֶתֶן תִּדְרֹךְ תִּרְמֹס כְּפִיר וְתַנִּין : 14 כִּי בִי חָשַׁק וַאֲפַלְּטֵהוּ אֲשַׂגְּבֵהוּ כִּי־יָדַע שְׁמִי : 15 יִקְרָאֵנִי וְאֶעֱנֵהוּ עִמֹּו־אָנֹכִי בְצָרָה אֲחַלְּצֵהוּ וַאֲכַבְּדֵהוּ : 16 אֹרֶךְ יָמִים אַשְׂבִּיעֵהוּ וְאַרְאֵהוּ בִּישׁוּעָתִי :

Even the Most High, [b]your dwelling place.

10 [a]No evil will befall you,
Nor will any plague come near your [1]tent.

Psa. 91:11 For He will give [a]His angels charge concerning you,
To guard you in all your ways.

12 They will [a]bear you up in their hands,
That you do not strike your foot against a stone.

13 You will [a]tread upon the lion and cobra,
The young lion and the [1]serpent you will trample down.

Psa. 91:14 "[a]Because he has loved Me, therefore I will deliver him;
I will [b]set him *securely* on high, because he has [c]known My name.

15 "He will [a]call upon Me, and I will answer him;
I will be with him in [1]trouble;
I will rescue him and [b]honor him.

16 "With [1]a [a]long life I will satisfy him
And [2][b]let him see My salvation."

References

Psalm 91:0
*a*Ps 27:5; 31:20; 32:7

Psalm 91:1
*b*Ps 17:8; 121:5; Is 25:4; 32:2

Psalm 91:2
*a*Ps 14:6; 91:9; 94:22; 142:5
*b*Ps 18:2; 31:3; Jer 16:19
*c*Ps 25:2; 56:4

Psalm 91:3
*a*Ps 124:7; Prov 6:5
*b*1 Kin 8:37; 2 Chr 20:9; Ps 91:6

Psalm 91:4
*a*Is 51:16
*b*Ps 17:8; 36:7; 57:1; 63:7
*c*Ps 40:11
*d*Ps 35:2

Psalm 91:5
*a*Job 5:19-23; Ps 23:4; 27:1
*b*Song 3:8
*c*Ps 64:4

Psalm 91:6
[1]Or *walks*
*a*2 Kin 19:35; Ps 91:10
*b*Job 5:22

Psalm 91:7
*a*Gen 7:23; Josh 14:10

Psalm 91:8
*a*Ps 37:34; 58:10

Psalm 91:9
[1]Or *For You O LORD are my Refuge; You have made the Most High your dwelling place*
[a]Ps 91:2
[b]Ps 90:1

Psalm 91:10
[1]Or *dwelling*
[a]Prov 12:21

Psalm 91:11
[a]Ps 34:7; Matt 4:6; Luke 4:10, 11; Heb 1:14

Psalm 91:12
[a]Matt 4:6; Luke 4:11

Psalm 91:13
[1]Or *dragon*
[a]Judg 14:6; Dan 6:22; Luke 10:19

Psalm 91:14
[a]Ps 145:20
[b]Ps 59:1
[c]Ps 9:10

Psalm 91:15
[1]Or *distress*
[a]Job 12:4; Ps 50:15
[b]1 Sam 2:30; John 12:26

Psalm 91:16
[1]Lit *length of days*
[2]Or *cause him to feast his eyes on*
[a]Deut 6:2; Ps 21:4; Prov 3:1, 2
[b]Ps 50:23[c]Ps 83:18; 93:4; 113:5

Targum

Psa. 92:1 A psalm and song that the first Adam uttered concerning the Sabbath day. [2] It is good to give thanks in the presence of the LORD, and to praise your name, O Most High. [3] To recount your goodness in the morning, and your truth in the nights, [4] According to the harp of ten strings, and according to the lyre, upon the murmuring of harps. [5] For you have made me glad, O LORD, by your works; I will rejoice in the works of your hands. [6] How great are your works, O LORD; your thoughts are very deep. [7] A foolish son of man will not know it, and a fool will not comprehend this. [8] While the wicked flourish like grass and all workers of deceit blossom, God is going to destroy them forever. [9] But you are high and supreme in this age, O LORD, and you are high and supreme in the age to come. [ANOTHER TARGUM: And you, your hand is supreme to punish the wicked in the age to come, in the great day of judgment, O LORD; and you, your hand is supreme to give a good reward to the righteous in the age to come, O LORD.] [10] For, behold, your enemies, O LORD, for behold, your enemies will perish in the age to come; and all the workers of deceit will be separated from the band of the righteous. [11] You have raised up my might like a wild-ox; you have anointed me with moist anointing oil of the leafy olive. [12] And my eye has looked on the perdition of my oppressors; my ear has heard the sound of the destruction of those who stand against me to do harm. [13] The righteous man will grow fruit like the palm-tree, like the cedar in Lebanon he will grow and produce roots. [14] His sons will be planted in the sanctuary of the LORD; in the court of the house of our God they will flourish. [15] Again like their fathers they will produce sons in old age; they will be plump and juicy. [16] So that the inhabitants of the earth might tell it, for the LORD is upright; my strength, and there is no wrong in him.

Spiritual Awareness

Introduction

This Psalm was composed by Moses and dedicated to the Levites. The Levites dwelled in the shadow of the LORD because they spent their days in the insulated and sacred environment of the Tabernacle and the Temple. Midrash says that Moses composed this work on the day he completed the construction of the Tabernacle. After its completion, Moses entered the Divine clouds and was enveloped by the shadow of the LORD.

Verse four

Pinions are the "spread-out wings" of a bird. The LORD will give you special consideration when you are an instrument of His. When you are under the pinions, you have a special relationship with the LORD. He will shelter you even as the mother bird shelters her young beneath her wings.

He will cover you with His pinions, and you will take refuge beneath His wings; His truth is a barbed shield and armor.

Notes of the Psalm

The rest of the Psalm describes everything the LORD will do to ensure nothing will harm the people under his pinion. When Israel stayed true to the Sinai covenant, the LORD spread His pinions and protected them. It is when they disobeyed the LORD's Law that the protection was removed. For today, it is imperative to follow the LORD's Law. This adherence will bring the LORD's protection.

Psalm 92

New American Standard 1995	Hebrew
Psa. 92:0 A Psalm, a Song for the Sabbath day. **Psa. 92:1** It is [a]good to give thanks to the LORD And to [b]sing praises to Your name, O Most High; 2 To [a]declare Your lovingkindness in the morning And Your [b]faithfulness [1]by night, 3 [1]With the [a]ten-stringed lute and [1]with the [a]harp, [1]With resounding music [2]upon the [a]lyre. 4 For You, O LORD, have made me glad by [1]what You [a]have done, I will [b]sing for joy at the [c]works of Your hands. **Psa. 92:5** How [a]great are Your works, O LORD! Your [1b]thoughts are very [c]deep. 6 A [a]senseless man has no knowledge, Nor does a [a]stupid man understand this: 7 That when the wicked [a]sprouted up like grass And all [b]who did iniquity flourished, It *was only* that they might be [c]destroyed forevermore. 8 But You, O LORD, are [a]on high forever.	מִזְמוֹר שִׁיר לְיוֹם הַשַּׁבָּת : ² **Psa. 92:1** טוֹב לְהֹדוֹת לַיהוָה וּלְזַמֵּר לְשִׁמְךָ עֶלְיוֹן : ³ לְהַגִּיד בַּבֹּקֶר חַסְדֶּךָ וֶאֱמוּנָתְךָ בַּלֵּילוֹת : ⁴ עֲלֵי־עָשׂוֹר וַעֲלֵי־נָבֶל עֲלֵי הִגָּיוֹן בְּכִנּוֹר : ⁵ כִּי שִׂמַּחְתַּנִי יְהוָה בְּפָעֳלֶךָ בְּמַעֲשֵׂי יָדֶיךָ אֲרַנֵּן : ⁶ מַה־גָּדְלוּ מַעֲשֶׂיךָ יְהוָה מְאֹד עָמְקוּ מַחְשְׁבֹתֶיךָ : ⁷ אִישׁ־בַּעַר לֹא יֵדָע וּכְסִיל לֹא־יָבִין אֶת־זֹאת : ⁸ בִּפְרֹחַ רְשָׁעִים כְּמוֹ עֵשֶׂב וַיָּצִיצוּ כָּל־פֹּעֲלֵי אָוֶן לְהִשָּׁמְדָם עֲדֵי־עַד : ⁹ וְאַתָּה מָרוֹם לְעֹלָם יְהוָה : ¹⁰ כִּי הִנֵּה אֹיְבֶיךָ | יְהוָה כִּי־הִנֵּה אֹיְבֶיךָ יֹאבֵדוּ יִתְפָּרְדוּ כָּל־פֹּעֲלֵי אָוֶן : ¹¹ וַתָּרֶם כִּרְאֵים קַרְנִי בַּלֹּתִי בְּשֶׁמֶן רַעֲנָן : ¹² וַתַּבֵּט עֵינִי בְּשׁוּרָי בַּקָּמִים עָלַי מְרֵעִים תִּשְׁמַעְנָה אָזְנָי : ¹³ צַדִּיק כַּתָּמָר יִפְרָח כְּאֶרֶז בַּלְּבָנוֹן יִשְׂגֶּה : ¹⁴ שְׁתוּלִים בְּבֵית יְהוָה בְּחַצְרוֹת אֱלֹהֵינוּ יַפְרִיחוּ : ¹⁵ עוֹד יְנוּבוּן בְּשֵׂיבָה דְּשֵׁנִים וְרַעֲנַנִּים יִהְיוּ : ¹⁶ לְהַגִּיד כִּי־יָשָׁר יְהוָה צוּרִי וְלֹא־ עֹלָתָה [עַוְלָתָה] בּוֹ :

⁹   For, behold, Your enemies, O LORD,

For, behold, ^{*a*}Your enemies will perish;

All who do iniquity will be ^{*b*}scattered.

Psa. 92:10   But You have exalted my ^{*a*}horn like *that of* the wild ox;

I have ¹been ^{*b*}anointed with fresh oil.

¹¹   And my eye has ^{*a*}looked *exultantly* upon ¹my foes,

My ears hear of the evildoers who rise up against me.

¹²   The ^{*a*}righteous man will ¹flourish like the palm tree,

He will grow like a ^{*b*}cedar in Lebanon.

¹³   ^{*a*}Planted in the house of the LORD,

They will flourish ^{*b*}in the courts of our God.

¹⁴   They will still ^{1*a*}yield fruit in old age;

They shall be ²full of sap and very green,

¹⁵   To ¹declare that ^{*a*}the LORD is upright;

He is my ^{*b*}rock, and there is ^{*c*}no unrighteousness in Him.

References

Psalm 92:1
[a]Ps 147:1
[b]Ps 135:3

Psalm 92:2
[1]Lit *nights*
[a]Ps 59:16
[b]Ps 89:1

Psalm 92:3
[1]Lit *Upon*
[2]Lit *by means of*
[a]1 Sam 10:5; 1 Chr 13:8; Neh 12:27; Ps 33:2

Psalm 92:4
[1]Lit *Your working*
[a]Ps 40:5; 90:16
[b]Ps 106:47
[c]Ps 8:6; 111:7; 143:5

Psalm 92:5
[1]Or *purposes*
[a]Ps 40:5; 111:2; Rev 15:3
[b]Ps 33:11; 40:5; 139:17
[c]Ps 36:6; Rom 11:33

Psalm 92:6
[a]Ps 49:10; 73:22; 94:8

Psalm 92:7
[a]Job 12:6; Ps 90:5
[b]Ps 94:4
[c]Ps 37:38

Psalm 92:8
[a]Ps 83:18; 93:4; 113:5

Psalm 92:9

[a]Ps 37:20
[b]Ps 68:1; 89:10

Psalm 92:10

[1]Or *become moist*
[a]Ps 75:10; 89:17; 112:9
[b]Ps 23:5; 45:7

Psalm 92:11

[1]Or *those who lie in wait for me*
[a]Ps 54:7; 91:8

Psalm 92:12

[1]Lit *sprout*
[a]Num 24:6; Ps 1:3; 52:8; 72:7; Jer 17:8; Hos 14:5, 6
[b]Ps 104:16; Ezek 31:3

Psalm 92:13

[a]Ps 80:15; Is 60:21
[b]Ps 100:4; 116:19

Psalm 92:14

[1]Or *thrive in*
[2]Lit *fat and*
[a]Prov 11:30; Is 37:31; John 15:2; James 3:18

Psalm 92:15

[1]Or *show forth*
[a]Job 34:10; Ps 25:8
[b]Deut 32:4; Ps 18:2; 94:22
[c]Rom 9:14

Targum

Psa. 92:1 A psalm and song that the first Adam uttered concerning the Sabbath day. ² It is good to give thanks in the presence of the LORD, and to praise your name, O Most High. ³ To recount your goodness in the morning, and your truth in the nights, ⁴ According to the harp of ten strings, and according to the lyre, upon the murmuring of harps. ⁵ For you have made me glad, O LORD, by your works; I will rejoice in the works of your hands. ⁶ How great are your works, O LORD; your thoughts are very deep. ⁷ A foolish son of man will not know it, and a fool will not comprehend this. ⁸ While the wicked flourish like grass and all workers of deceit blossom, God is going to destroy them forever. ⁹ But you are high and supreme in this age, O LORD, and you are high and supreme in the age to come. [ANOTHER TARGUM: And you, your hand is supreme to punish the wicked in the age to come, in the great day of judgment, O LORD; and you, your hand is supreme to give a good reward to the righteous in the age to come, O LORD.] ¹⁰ For, behold, your enemies, O LORD, for behold, your enemies will perish in the age to come; and all the workers of deceit will be separated from the band of the righteous. ¹¹ You have raised up my might like a wild-ox; you have anointed me with moist anointing oil of the leafy olive. ¹² And my eye has looked on the perdition of my oppressors; my ear has heard the sound of the destruction of those who stand against me to do harm. ¹³ The righteous man will grow fruit like the palm-tree, like the cedar in Lebanon he will grow and produce roots. ¹⁴ His sons will be planted in the sanctuary of the LORD; in the court of the house of our God they will flourish. ¹⁵ Again like their fathers they will produce sons in old age; they will be plump and juicy. ¹⁶ So that the inhabitants of the earth might tell it, for the LORD is upright; my strength, and there is no wrong in him.

Spiritual Awareness

Introduction

The LORD completed physical creation in six days. The spiritual creation of humanity will continue until the world ends. It is unfair to judge God's equity before the denouement of human history, even though history appears to be a long series of tragic injustices. Each injustice has hopefully taught a lesson to humanity that is carried to the next generation.

On the first Shabbat, Adam surveyed the LORD's completed work and was stirred to sing of the marvelous perfection his eyes beheld. This Psalm speaks of man's bewilderment as he observes the apparent inequity in the world. It also tells of the joy he will experience when the inequities are resolved.

Verse two

To proclaim the work of the Sefirah Chesed in the morning and Your faithfulness in the nights.

Verse seven

There are evil people on earth who do not understand that materialism is only one-half of human existence. These people only believe what they can touch. Faith in the LORD requires a person to believe in something that cannot be seen, but the person knows it is there.

When the lawless spring up as the grass, where all the abusers of might flourish, that is so that they may be destroyed forever.

Verse ten

The LORD does not have to intervene with a supernatural act to destroy wicked people. The LORD wrote their destruction into the Torah, which created the Universe's fabric. Each person will have to answer for the sins they did not repent. It is best to repent for sins committed before it is too late. When the flesh dies, the rest of the soul must answer for sins. One will not have the opportunity in the LORD's court to ask for forgiveness or another chance to repent.

While you lifted by my horns like that of the wild ox, I outlive them with ever-renewed consecration.

Verse thirteen

Grass will grow anywhere by itself. Palm and cedar trees which the righteous person is compared to here, are planted deliberately in the House of the LORD. The fruit is the mitzvot that the righteous perform in the name of the LORD.

Planted in the House of God, they will flourish in the courts of our God.

Psalm 93

New American Standard 1995	Hebrew
Psa. 93:1 *The LORD [1]reigns, He is *clothed with majesty; The LORD has *clothed and girded Himself with strength; Indeed, the *world is firmly established, it will not be moved. 2 Your *throne is established from of old; You *are from everlasting. **Psa. 93:3** The *floods have lifted up, O LORD, The floods have lifted up their voice, The floods lift up their pounding waves. 4 More than the sounds of many waters, *Than* the mighty breakers of the sea, The LORD *on high is mighty. 5 Your *testimonies are fully confirmed; *Holiness befits Your house, O LORD, [1]forevermore.	**Psa. 93:1** יְהוָה מָלָךְ גֵּאוּת לָבֵשׁ לָבֵשׁ יְהוָה עֹז הִתְאַזָּר אַף־תִּכּוֹן תֵּבֵל בַּל־תִּמּוֹט: 2 נָכוֹן כִּסְאֲךָ מֵאָז מֵעוֹלָם אָתָּה: 3 נָשְׂאוּ נְהָרוֹת יְהוָה נָשְׂאוּ נְהָרוֹת קוֹלָם יִשְׂאוּ נְהָרוֹת דָּכְיָם: 4 מִקֹּלוֹת מַיִם רַבִּים אַדִּירִים מִשְׁבְּרֵי־יָם אַדִּיר בַּמָּרוֹם יְהוָה: 5 עֵדֹתֶיךָ נֶאֶמְנוּ מְאֹד לְבֵיתְךָ נַאֲוָה־קֹדֶשׁ יְהוָה לְאֹרֶךְ יָמִים:

References

Psalm 93:1

[1]Or *has assumed kingship*
[a]Ps 96:10; 97:1; 99:1
[b]Ps 104:1
[c]Ps 65:6; Is 51:9
[d]Ps 96:10

Psalm 93:2

[a]Ps 45:6; Lam 5:19
[b]Ps 90:2

Psalm 93:3

[a]Ps 96:11; 98:7, 8

Psalm 93:4

[a]Ps 65:7; 89:6, 9; 92:8

Psalm 93:5

[1]Lit *for length of days*
[a]Ps 19:7
[b]Ps 29:2; 96:9; 1 Cor 3:17

Targum

Psa. 93:1 The LORD is king, he has put on greatness; the LORD has put on strength and girded himself; also he made strong the world, so that it will not be shaken. ² Your throne is established from the beginning; from eternity you are God. ³ The rivers lift up, O LORD, the rivers lift up their voice in song; the rivers will receive a reward for their praise. ⁴ The LORD is more to be praised in the highest heavens than the sound of many waters, the praiseworthy [waters], the breakers of the great sea! ⁵ Your testimonies are very true, beautiful and holy for your sanctuary, O LORD, for length of days.

Spiritual Awareness

Introduction

The sage Rashi explained that this Psalm is dedicated to the Messianic era when all men will recognize the LORD's majesty again. It is a continuation of Psalm 92, which concluded with the prediction that people will declare the LORD just in the Messianic era. All humanity will recognize the LORD as the true God of Heaven and earth.

This Psalm is the song of the day for the sixth day of the week because the LORD completed his work on that day. Rav Yaakov Emden said this Psalm describes the LORD as robing himself in grandeur like one dressing in high Sabbath finery. On the sixth day, Adam was created. The LORD blew a breath of life into his nostrils and invested him with a Divine soul. As Adam sang praises to the LORD, he honestly looked Divine because he was a reflection of the LORD. All the creators of creation gathered to bow to him in submission because they thought Adam was their creator.

Verse three

"Floods" is a simile for powerful nations that swell with pride and work destruction in the world. These nations are hostile to the LORD's supremacy and have noisily raised their voices. In time they will be destroyed.

True, the floods, O LORD, the floods have lifted up their voices; the floods lift up their fall.

Psalm 94

New American Standard 1995	Hebrew
Psa. 94:1 O LORD, God of [1a]vengeance, God of [1]vengeance, [2b]shine forth! [2] [a]Rise up, O [b]Judge of the earth, Render recompense [c]to the proud. [3] How long shall the wicked, O LORD, How long shall the [a]wicked exult? [4] They pour forth *words,* they [a]speak arrogantly; All who do wickedness [b]vaunt themselves. [5] They [a]crush Your people, O LORD, And [b]afflict Your heritage. [6] They [a]slay the widow and the [1]stranger And murder the orphans. [7] [a]They have said, "[1]The LORD does not see, Nor does the God of Jacob pay heed." **Psa. 94:8** Pay heed, you [a]senseless among the people; And when will you understand, [a]stupid ones? [9] He who [a]planted the ear, [1]does He not hear? He who formed the eye, [1]does He not see? [10] He who [1a]chastens the nations, will He not rebuke, *Even* He who [b]teaches man knowledge?	אֵל־נְקָמוֹת יְהוָה אֵל **Psa 94**:1 נְקָמוֹת הוֹפִיעַ ׃ ² הִנָּשֵׂא שֹׁפֵט הָאָרֶץ הָשֵׁב גְּמוּל עַל־גֵּאִים ׃ ³ עַד־מָתַי רְשָׁעִים ׀ יְהוָה עַד־מָתַי רְשָׁעִים יַעֲלֹזוּ ׃ ⁴ יַבִּיעוּ יְדַבְּרוּ עָתָק יִתְאַמְּרוּ כָּל־פֹּעֲלֵי אָוֶן ׃ ⁵ עַמְּךָ יְהוָה יְדַכְּאוּ וְנַחֲלָתְךָ יְעַנּוּ ׃ ⁶ אַלְמָנָה וְגֵר יַהֲרֹגוּ וִיתוֹמִים יְרַצֵּחוּ ׃ ⁷ וַיֹּאמְרוּ לֹא יִרְאֶה־יָּהּ וְלֹא־יָבִין אֱלֹהֵי יַעֲקֹב ׃ ⁸ בִּינוּ בֹּעֲרִים בָּעָם וּכְסִילִים מָתַי תַּשְׂכִּילוּ ׃ ⁹ הֲנֹטַע אֹזֶן הֲלֹא יִשְׁמָע אִם־יֹצֵר עַיִן הֲלֹא יַבִּיט ׃ ¹⁰ הֲיֹסֵר גּוֹיִם הֲלֹא יוֹכִיחַ הַמְלַמֵּד אָדָם דָּעַת ׃ ¹¹ יְהוָה יֹדֵעַ מַחְשְׁבוֹת אָדָם כִּי־הֵמָּה הָבֶל ׃ ¹² אַשְׁרֵי ׀ הַגֶּבֶר אֲשֶׁר־תְּיַסְּרֶנּוּ יָּהּ וּמִתּוֹרָתְךָ תְלַמְּדֶנּוּ ׃ ¹³ לְהַשְׁקִיט לוֹ מִימֵי רָע עַד יִכָּרֶה לָרָשָׁע שָׁחַת ׃ ¹⁴ כִּי ׀ לֹא־ יִטֹּשׁ יְהוָה עַמּוֹ וְנַחֲלָתוֹ לֹא יַעֲזֹב ׃ ¹⁵ כִּי־עַד־צֶדֶק יָשׁוּב מִשְׁפָּט וְאַחֲרָיו כָּל־יִשְׁרֵי־לֵב ׃ ¹⁶ מִי־יָקוּם לִי עִם־מְרֵעִים מִי־יִתְיַצֵּב לִי עִם־ פֹּעֲלֵי אָוֶן ׃ ¹⁷ לוּלֵי יְהוָה עֶזְרָתָה לִּי כִּמְעַט ׀ שָׁכְנָה דוּמָה נַפְשִׁי ׃ ¹⁸ אִם־

11 The LORD ^aknows the thoughts of man,

¹That they are a *mere* breath.

Psa. 94:12 Blessed is the man whom ^aYou chasten, O ¹LORD,

And ^bwhom You teach out of Your law;

13 That You may grant him ^arelief from the ^bdays of adversity,

Until ^ca pit is dug for the wicked.

14 For ^athe LORD will not abandon His people,

Nor will He ^bforsake His inheritance.

15 For ^{1a}judgment ²will again be righteous,

And all the upright in heart ³will follow it.

16 Who will ^astand up for me against evildoers?

Who will take his stand for me ^bagainst those who do wickedness?

Psa. 94:17 If ^athe LORD had not been my help,

My soul would soon have dwelt in *the abode of* silence.

18 If I should say, "^aMy foot has slipped,"

Your loving-kindness, O LORD, will hold me up.

19 When my anxious thoughts ¹multiply within me,

Your ^aconsolations delight my soul.

20 Can a ^{1a}throne of destruction be allied with You,

One ^bwhich devises ²mischief by decree?

אָמַרְתִּי מָטָה רַגְלִי חַסְדְּךָ יְהֹוָה

יִסְעָדֵנִי ׃ 19 בְּרֹב שַׂרְעַפַּי בְּקִרְבִּי

תַּנְחוּמֶיךָ יְשַׁעַשְׁעוּ נַפְשִׁי ׃ 20

הַיְחָבְרְךָ כִּסֵּא הַוּוֹת יֹצֵר עָמָל

עֲלֵי־חֹק ׃ 21 יָגוֹדוּ עַל־נֶפֶשׁ צַדִּיק

וְדָם נָקִי יַרְשִׁיעוּ ׃ 22 וַיְהִי יְהֹוָה לִי

לְמִשְׂגָּב וֵאלֹהַי לְצוּר מַחְסִי ׃ 23

וַיָּשֶׁב עֲלֵיהֶם ׀ אֶת־אוֹנָם וּבְרָעָתָם

יַצְמִיתֵם יַצְמִיתֵם יְהֹוָה אֱלֹהֵינוּ ׃

21 They *a*band themselves together against the [1]life of the righteous

And *b*condemn [2]the innocent to death.

22 But the LORD has been my *a*stronghold,

And my God the *b*rock of my refuge.

23 He has *a*brought back their wickedness upon them

And will [1]*b*destroy them in their evil;

The LORD our God will [1]destroy them.

References

Psalm 94:1
[1]Or *avenging acts*
[2]Or *has shone forth*
[a]Deut 32:35; Is 35:4; Nah 1:2; Rom 12:19
[b]Ps 50:2; 80:1

Psalm 94:2
[a]Ps 7:6
[b]Gen 18:25
[c]Ps 31:23

Psalm 94:3
[a]Job 20:5

Psalm 94:4
[a]Ps 31:18; 75:5
[b]Ps 10:3; 52:1

Psalm 94:5
[a]Is 3:15
[b]Ps 79:1

Psalm 94:6
[1]Or *sojourner*
[a]Is 10:2

Psalm 94:7
[1]Heb *YAH*
[a]Job 22:13; Ps 10:11

Psalm 94:8
[a]Ps 92:6

Psalm 94:9

[1]Or *can*
[a]Ex 4:11; Prov 20:12

Psalm 94:10
[1]Or *instructs*
[a]Ps 44:2
[b]Job 35:11; Is 28:26

Psalm 94:11
[1]Or *For*
[a]Job 11:11; 1 Cor 3:20

Psalm 94:12
[1]Heb *YAH*
[a]Deut 8:5; Job 5:17; Ps 119:71; Prov 3:11, 12; Heb 12:5, 6
[b]Ps 119:171

Psalm 94:13
[a]Job 34:29; Hab 3:16
[b]Ps 49:5
[c]Ps 9:15; 55:23

Psalm 94:14
[a]1 Sam 12:22; Lam 3:31; Rom 11:2
[b]Ps 37:28

Psalm 94:15
[1]I.e. administration of justice
[2]Lit *will return to righteousness*
[3]Lit *will be after it*
[a]Ps 97:2; Is 42:3; Mic 7:9

Psalm 94:16
[a]Num 10:35; Is 28:21; 33:10
[b]Ps 17:13; 59:2

Psalm 94:17
*a*Ps 124:1, 2

Psalm 94:18
*a*Ps 38:16; 73:2

Psalm 94:19
[1]Or *are many*
*a*Is 57:18; 66:13

Psalm 94:20
[1]Or *tribunal*
[2]Or *trouble, misfortune*
*a*Amos 6:3
*b*Ps 50:16; 58:2

Psalm 94:21
[1]Or *soul*
[2]Lit *innocent blood*
*a*Ps 56:6; 59:3
*b*Ex 23:7; Ps 106:38; Prov 17:15; Matt 27:4

Psalm 94:22
*a*Ps 9:9; 59:9
*b*Ps 18:2; 71:7

Targum

Psa. 94:1 The God who takes vengeance is the LORD; the God who takes vengeance has appeared. **2** Lift yourself up, O judge of the earth; requite evil to the proud. **3** How long will the wicked, O LORD, how long will the wicked dwell in tranquillity? **4** They will gush and speak blasphemy; all the workers of deceit utter disgraceful words. **5** They will crush your people, O LORD, and impoverish your inheritance. **6** They will kill the widow and proselyte, and they will murder orphans. **7** And they said, "Yah will not see, and the God of Jacob will not comprehend it." **8** Consider, you who are fools among the people; and you unwise – when will you gain insight? **9** Could it be that the ear was planted, and hears no instruction? Or could it be that he created the eye, and it has not looked at the Torah? **10** Could it be that he gave the Torah to his people, and when they sin, they are not rebuked? Did not the LORD teach knowledge to the first Adam? **11** The thoughts of the sons of men are known in the presence of the LORD, for they are nothingness. **12** It is well for the man whom you rebuke, O Yah; and you will instruct him out of your Torah. **13** To give him quietness from the days of evil until the pit is created for the wicked. **14** For the LORD will not abandon his people, nor will he forsake his inheritance. **15** For justice will return to righteousness, and after it all the upright of heart will be redeemed. **16** Who will arise for me to do battle with evildoers? Who will stand up for me to dispute with workers of deceit? **17** If the LORD were not my helper, my soul would almost have dwelt in silence. **18** If I said, "My foot is slipping," your goodness, O LORD, will aid me. **19** In the many thoughts within me, your comforts will delight my soul. **20** Could it be that the throne of deceit will be allied with you? Or could the creature of toil stand against the covenant? **21** Evil things will gather against the soul of the righteous man; and they will condemn innocent blood to the judgment of death. **22** But the LORD will be a helper for me; and my God is the strength of my confidence.

[23] And he has turned their lies against them, and he will destroy them in their evil; the LORD our God will destroy them.

Spiritual Awareness

Introduction

This Psalm is the fifth of eleven Psalms written by Moses. This Psalm was dedicated to the tribe of Gad. Gad was renowned for its military prowess and ability to punish Israel's enemies, especially those that attacked her. The Midrash Shocher Tov Psalm 90 says that the prophet Elijah was from the tribe of Gad. It will be Elijah who brings the advent of the Messianic era. The LORD will appear as the God of vengeance. He will punish the proud and cruel nations (according to the sage Radak). The Talmud (Rosh Hashanah 31a) designates this Psalm as the Song of the Day for the fourth day of the week. This day is when the LORD created the sun and moon. The God of vengeance will punish the idolaters who worshiped these celestial bodies. Moses composed this Psalm as a prayer to bring the day of the Messianic redemption and retribution closer (according to the sage Radak).

Verse one

אֵל־נְקָמֹות (el-n'chamot) means "God of vengeance." This name of the LORD also denotes "champion of justice." Israel had a difficult time with the nations that wanted to destroy her. The Jewish people have been in exile and persecution since the Babylonian invasion of Judah. The Holocaust is an example of human cruelty to people devoted to the LORD. In the Messianic era, these nations will be held responsible for what they did and are doing to the Jewish people. The God of vengeance will ensure that they are sent to Sheol and will never be able to hurt Israel again.

LORD, champion of justice, God of vengeance, shine forth.

Verse eighteen

The Psalmist calls out to the Sefirah Chesed for the LORD's loving-kindness.

Whenever I said, "My foot has slipped," You send power from the Sefirah Chesed, O LORD upheld me.

Notes of the Psalm

This Psalm addresses a problem that several other Psalms have addressed and is a question today. Why can evil people thrive in the world? Should not the LORD step in and do something about it? In a materialistic world, people will always rise to a position of power or wealth because they have taken advantage of others. It is evident in American politics. There is also an elite class of people who have obtained their wealth and prestige on the backs of what they call lower-class people. Today the elite are trying to prevent anyone trying to rise from the lower classes from entering the elite. These people loved capitalism and democracy while they built their wealth and power. Today the World Economic council is filled with these people. They do not want new blood in the group because they can show the world the group's true mission. This group is trying to control the world.

The Psalmist asks the LORD why He has not stepped in. The LORD despises people who exploit their brothers and sisters to become powerful and wealthy. To the average person, the LORD appears to remain outside the situation. The answer is that one day the LORD will decide that He has witnessed enough. He hears the cries of the non-elite and will, in His time, send the God of vengeance through the Sefirah Gevurah. That is the beginning of the Messianic era. People holding the world hostage, the world's elites, will be destroyed and sent to Sheol. The average person will be given a chance to live in a world where everyone can prosper and enjoy.

Moses knew that an elite group would form in the world. Thus, he wrote this Psalm to give hope to the people who are not elite. One day the LORD will correct this situation.

Psalm 95

New American Standard 1995	Hebrew

Psa. 95:1   O come, let us *a*sing for joy to the LORD,
   Let us shout joyfully to *b*the rock of our salvation.
2   Let us *a*come before His presence *b*with [1]thanksgiving,
   Let us shout joyfully to Him *c*with [2]psalms.
3   For the LORD is a *a*great God
   And a great King *b*above all gods,
4   In whose hand are the *a*depths of the earth,
   The peaks of the mountains are His also.
5   [1]The sea is His, for it was He *a*who made it,
   And His hands formed the dry land.
 	
Psa. 95:6   Come, let us *a*worship and bow down,
   Let us *b*kneel before the LORD our *c*Maker.
7   For He is our God,
   And *a*we are the people of His [1b]pasture and the sheep of His hand.
   *c*Today, [2]if you would hear His voice,
8   Do not harden your hearts, as at [1a]Meribah,
   As in the day of [2b]Massah in the wilderness,
9   "When your fathers *a*tested Me,
   They tried Me, though they had seen My work.
	לְכוּ נְרַנְּנָה לַיהוָה נָרִיעָה **Psa. 95:1**
	לְצוּר יִשְׁעֵנוּ ׃ ² נְקַדְּמָה פָנָיו
	בְּתוֹדָה בִּזְמִרוֹת נָרִיעַ לוֹ ׃ ³ כִּי אֵל
	גָּדוֹל יְהוָה וּמֶלֶךְ גָּדוֹל עַל־כָּל־
	אֱלֹהִים ׃ ⁴ אֲשֶׁר בְּיָדוֹ מֶחְקְרֵי־אָרֶץ
	וְתוֹעֲפוֹת הָרִים לוֹ ׃ ⁵ אֲשֶׁר־לוֹ הַיָּם
	וְהוּא עָשָׂהוּ וְיַבֶּשֶׁת יָדָיו יָצָרוּ ׃ ⁶
	בֹּאוּ נִשְׁתַּחֲוֶה וְנִכְרָעָה נִבְרְכָה
	לִפְנֵי־יְהוָה עֹשֵׂנוּ ׃ ⁷ כִּי הוּא
	אֱלֹהֵינוּ וַאֲנַחְנוּ עַם מַרְעִיתוֹ וְצֹאן
	יָדוֹ הַיּוֹם אִם־בְּקֹלוֹ תִשְׁמָעוּ ׃ ⁸
	אַל־תַּקְשׁוּ לְבַבְכֶם כִּמְרִיבָה כְּיוֹם
	מַסָּה בַּמִּדְבָּר ׃ ⁹ אֲשֶׁר נִסּוּנִי
	אֲבוֹתֵיכֶם בְּחָנוּנִי גַּם־רָאוּ פָעֳלִי ׃ ¹⁰
	אַרְבָּעִים שָׁנָה אָקוּט בְּדוֹר וָאֹמַר
	עַם תֹּעֵי לֵבָב הֵם וְהֵם לֹא־יָדְעוּ
	דְרָכָי ׃ ¹¹ אֲשֶׁר־נִשְׁבַּעְתִּי בְאַפִּי
	אִם־יְבֹאוּן אֶל־מְנוּחָתִי ׃

10   "For ^aforty years I loathed *that* generation,
      And said they are a people who err in their heart,
      And they do not know My ways.
11   "Therefore I ^aswore in My anger,
      Truly they shall not enter into My ^brest."	

References

Psalm 95:1
[a]Ps 66:1; 81:1
[b]Ps 89:26

Psalm 95:2
[1]Or *a song of thanksgiving*
[2]Or *songs* (with instrumental accompaniment)
[a]Mic 6:6
[b]Ps 100:4; 147:7; Jon 2:9
[c]Ps 81:2; Eph 5:19; James 5:13

Psalm 95:3
[a]Ps 48:1; 135:5; 145:3
[b]Ps 96:4; 97:9

Psalm 95:4
[a]Ps 135:6

Psalm 95:5
[1]Lit *Who has the sea*
[a]Gen 1:9, 10; Ps 146:6; Jon 1:9

Psalm 95:6
[a]Ps 96:9; 99:5, 9
[b]2 Chr 6:13; Dan 6:10; Phil 2:10
[c]Ps 100:3; 149:2; Is 17:7; Hos 8:14

Psalm 95:7
[1]Lit *pasturing*
[2]Or *O that you would obey*
[a]Ps 79:13
[b]Ps 74:1
[c]Heb 3:7-11, 15; 4:7

Psalm 95:8
[1]Or *place of strife*
[2]Or *temptation*
[a]Ex 17:2-7; Num 20:13

[b]Ex 17:7; Deut 6:16

Psalm 95:9
[a]Num 14:22; Ps 78:18; 1 Cor 10:9

Psalm 95:10
[a]Acts 7:36; 13:18; Heb 3:10, 17

Psalm 95:11
[a]Num 14:23, 28-30; Deut 1:35; Heb 4:3, 5
[b]Deut 12:9

Targum

Psa. 95:1 Come, let us sing praise before the LORD, let us shout aloud before the Mighty One of our redemption. [2] Let us come before his face with thanksgiving, with hymns let us shout aloud before him. [3] For the LORD is the great God, and the great king over every god. [4] From whose hand the depths of the earth are suspended, and the strongholds of the mountain height are his. [5] His is the sea, and he made it; and his hands created the dry land. [6] Come, let us bow down and prostrate ourselves; let us kneel in the presence of the LORD who makes us. [7] For he is our God and we are his people and the flock of his hand's pasturing; today, if you accept his word – [8] Do not harden your heart as in the dispute, as on the day you tested God in the wilderness. [9] For your fathers tempted me, they tried me; yet they saw my works. [10] Forty years I rejected the generation of the wilderness, and I said, "They are a people with error in their heart, and they do not know my ways." [11] For I swore in the harshness of my wrath, "They will not enter the repose of my sanctuary."

Spiritual Awareness

Introduction

This Psalm is the sixth Psalm of eleven composed by Moses. It is dedicated to the tribe of Issachar. She was a tribe of scholars who were constantly immersed in the joyous songs of the Torah. The Psalm is divided into two sections. The first seven verses are a call to the psalmist's people. He calls them to sing to the LORD and praise Him. The second section is a direct exhortation from the LORD to Israel. The psalmist recalls the disastrous results of our ancestor's sin in the Sinai Wilderness and urges us not to emulate that course of action.

Verse seven

The LORD's pasture is where the motivation for the emotion of love for the LORD takes over a person. A joyous mood with songs of thanksgiving is sung to the LORD. It is a place of perfect devotion.

For He is our God and we are the people of His pastures and the flock of His hand, even today, if you will but harken to His Voice.

Verse eight

"Meribah was a site that the Israelites passed through in their desert wanderings. Being a place of testing for the Israelites, it also had a major impact in the lives of Moses and Aaron. Apparently, based on the biblical text, there are two sites named Meribah (W. A. Elwell and B. J. Beitzel, "Meribah," *Baker Encyclopedia of the Bible*, volume 2, Baker, 1988, p. 1,442). One of the sites called Meribah was located near Rephidim in the Desert of Sin (Exodus 17:1). At this location it was also called Massah, which differentiates it from the other Meribah mentioned in Scripture (Deuteronomy 6:16; 9:22; 33:8; Psalm 95:8). The other site named Meribah was located in Kadesh Barnea, and therefore was referred to as Meribah Kadesh (Numbers 27:14; Deuteronomy 32:51; Ezekiel 47:19; 48:28)."[1]

Harden not your heart, as at Merbiah, as on the day of the testing in the wilderness.

Verse eleven

The wandering of Israel in the Wilderness was a test from the LORD. Was Israel going to learn to trust the LORD? Moses sent spies into the Promised Land. Ten spies gave adverse reports when they returned and said it would be foolish to enter the land. Two spies, Joshua and Caleb, said that even though the people were strong, Israel would defeat them with the help of the LORD. The decision was made not to go into the land. Israel failed the test and spent forty years in the desert because of this error. Today God's people need to learn how to trust the direction of the LORD. One problem is the interpretation of the messages the LORD is sending to us. The division between Judaism and Christianity proves that neither group interprets the LORD's messages properly. Unity is an essential component that the LORD desires. For Judaism today, the majority of souls are kissing cousins. Therefore, Judaism can be viewed as one large extended family. Each member must learn to love the other. For the Christians, Jesus said that by being baptized into his name, all become a family. Perhaps it is fair to say both families are dysfunctional now.

So that I swore in My wrath: "They shall not enter into My rest."

---

[1] GotQuestions.org, "Home," GotQuestions.org, May 11, 2020, https://www.gotquestions.org/Meribah-in-the-Bible.html.

Psalm 96

New American Standard 1995	Hebrew

Psa. 96:1 *[a]*Sing to the LORD a *[b]*new song;

Sing to the LORD, all the earth.

2 Sing to the LORD, bless His name;

*[a]*Proclaim good tidings of His salvation from day to day.

3 Tell of *[a]*His glory among the nations,

His wonderful deeds among all the peoples.

4 For *[a]*great is the LORD and *[b]*greatly to be praised;

He is to be *[c]*feared *[d]*above all gods.

5 For *[a]*all the gods of the peoples are [1]idols,

But *[b]*the LORD made the heavens.

6 *[a]*Splendor and majesty are before Him,

Strength and beauty are in His sanctuary.

Psa. 96:7 [1]Ascribe to the LORD, O *[a]*families of the peoples,

[1][b]Ascribe to the LORD glory and strength.

8 [1]Ascribe to the LORD the *[a]*glory of His name;

Bring an [2][b]offering and come into His courts.

9 *[a]*Worship the LORD in [1]holy attire;

*[b]*Tremble before Him, all the earth.

10 Say among the nations, "*[a]*The LORD reigns;

Indeed, the *[a]*world is firmly established, it will not be moved;

שִׁירוּ לַיהוָה שִׁיר חָדָשׁ ‏**Psa. 96:1**

שִׁירוּ לַיהוָה כָּל־הָאָרֶץ ׃ ‏2 שִׁירוּ

לַיהוָה בָּרְכוּ שְׁמוֹ בַּשְּׂרוּ מִיּוֹם־

לְיוֹם יְשׁוּעָתוֹ ׃ ‏3 סַפְּרוּ בַגּוֹיִם

כְּבוֹדוֹ בְּכָל־הָעַמִּים נִפְלְאוֹתָיו ׃ ‏4

כִּי גָדוֹל יְהוָה וּמְהֻלָּל מְאֹד נוֹרָא

הוּא עַל־כָּל־אֱלֹהִים ׃ ‏5 כִּי ׀ כָּל־

אֱלֹהֵי הָעַמִּים אֱלִילִים וַיהוָה

שָׁמַיִם עָשָׂה ׃ ‏6 הוֹד־וְהָדָר לְפָנָיו

עֹז וְתִפְאֶרֶת בְּמִקְדָּשׁוֹ ׃ ‏7 הָבוּ

לַיהוָה מִשְׁפְּחוֹת עַמִּים הָבוּ לַיהוָה

כָּבוֹד וָעֹז ׃ ‏8 הָבוּ לַיהוָה כְּבוֹד

שְׁמוֹ שְׂאוּ־מִנְחָה וּבֹאוּ לְחַצְרוֹתָיו ׃

9 הִשְׁתַּחֲווּ לַיהוָה בְּהַדְרַת־קֹדֶשׁ

חִילוּ מִפָּנָיו כָּל־הָאָרֶץ ׃ ‏10 אִמְרוּ

בַגּוֹיִם ׀ יְהוָה מָלָךְ אַף־תִּכּוֹן תֵּבֵל

בַּל־תִּמּוֹט יָדִין עַמִּים בְּמֵישָׁרִים ׃ ‏11

יִשְׂמְחוּ הַשָּׁמַיִם וְתָגֵל הָאָרֶץ יִרְעַם

הַיָּם וּמְלֹאוֹ ׃ ‏12 יַעֲלֹז שָׂדַי וְכָל־

אֲשֶׁר־בּוֹ אָז יְרַנְּנוּ כָּל־עֲצֵי־יָעַר ׃ ‏13

לִפְנֵי יְהוָה ׀ כִּי בָא כִּי בָא לִשְׁפֹּט

הָאָרֶץ יִשְׁפֹּט־תֵּבֵל בְּצֶדֶק וְעַמִּים

בֶּאֱמוּנָתוֹ ׃

He will [b]judge the peoples with [1]equity."

Psa. 96:11 Let the [a]heavens be glad,
and let the [b]earth rejoice;
  Let [c]the sea [1]roar, and [2]all it contains;
[12]   Let the [a]field exult, and all that is in it.
  Then all the [b]trees of the forest will sing for joy
[13]   Before the LORD, [a]for He is coming,
  For He is coming to judge the earth.
  [b]He will judge the world in righteousness
  And the peoples in His faithfulness.

References

Psalm 96:1
[a]1 Chr 16:23-33
[b]Ps 40:3

Psalm 96:2
[a]Ps 71:15

Psalm 96:3
[a]Ps 145:12

Psalm 96:4
[a]Ps 48:1; 145:3
[b]Ps 18:3
[c]Ps 89:7
[d]Ps 95:3

Psalm 96:5
[1]Or *non-existent things*
[a]1 Chr 16:26; Jer 10:11
[b]Ps 115:15; Is 42:5

Psalm 96:6
[a]Ps 104:1

Psalm 96:7
[1]Lit *Give*
[a]Ps 22:27
[b]1 Chr 16:28, 29; Ps 29:1, 2

Psalm 96:8
[1]Lit *Give*
[2]Or *meal offering*
[a]Ps 79:9; 115:1

[b]Ps 45:12; 72:10

Psalm 96:9
[1]Or *the splendor of holiness*
[a]1 Chr 16:29; 2 Chr 20:21; Ps 29:2; 110:3
[b]Ps 33:8; 114:7

Psalm 96:10
[1]Or *uprightness*
[a]Ps 93:1; 97:1
[b]Ps 9:8; 58:11; 67:4; 98:9

Psalm 96:11
[1]Or *thunder*
[2]Lit *its fullness*
[a]Ps 69:34; Is 49:13
[b]Ps 97:1
[c]Ps 98:7

Psalm 96:12
[a]Ps 65:13; Is 35:1; 55:12, 13
[b]Is 44:23

Psalm 96:13
[a]Ps 98:9
[b]Rev 19:11

Targum

Psa. 96:1 Sing in the presence of the LORD a new psalm; sing praise, angels of the height, sing praise in the presence of the LORD, all righteous of the earth. **2** Sing praise in the presence of the LORD, bless his name; proclaim his redemption from day to day. **3** Tell of his glory among the Gentiles, of his wonders among all the peoples. **4** For great is the LORD and greatly to be praised; and he is more to be feared than any god. **5** For all the things feared by the Gentiles are idols; but the LORD made the heavens. **6** Praise and splendor are in his presence; strength and praise are in his sanctuary. **7** Make music in the presence of the LORD, O races of peoples; ascribe glory and strength in the presence of the LORD. **8** Ascribe glory in the presence of the LORD, and exalt his name; carry and bring an offering and enter his presence in his courts. **9** Bow down before him in the splendor of holiness; tremble in his presence, all inhabitants of the earth. **10** Say among the Gentiles, "The LORD reigns"; also the world is made firm that it will not totter; he will judge the peoples uprightly. **11** The forces of heaven will rejoice and the righteous of the earth will exult; the sea will shout and all its fullness. **12** The field and everything in it will pour forth praise; then all the trees of the forest will sing – **13** In the presence of the LORD, for he comes, for he comes to judge the earth; he will judge the world with righteousness and the peoples with his faithfulness.

Spiritual Awareness

Introduction

This Psalm is the seventh Psalm composed by Moses. Ibn Yachya[2] attempted to identify the tribes of the five remaining Psalms of Moses. He believed this Psalm was dedicated to Zebulun, who rejoiced when he went out to earn a livelihood so his brother Issachar could study the Torah. Zebulun would constantly sing to the LORD a new song thanking Him for the Divine blessing which resulted from his wealth.

David adapted this Psalm to his circumstances. The sage Radak believed that David did this when the Ark of the Covenant returned from exile in Philista. When Israel is released from exile, the Jews will join the Messiah and exult: Sing to HaShem a new song to Hashem to everyone on earth.

Notes to the Psalm

Verses four and five show that the idea of monotheism had not yet spread across the earth. The God of Israel was the God who created Heaven and Earth. However, the LORD was not the God of all nations yet. Each nation had its own gods. These were false gods, and worshiping them was idolatry. The psalmist says that eventually, all nations of the world will come to know the LORD and that the LORD is the only God of Heaven and Earth because He created all things.

---

[2] 16th century Bible commentator, a member of the famous Ibn Yachia family which produced many great Torah scholars. He composed a commentary on the Five Megilot, and a book on Gan Eden and the afterlife called "Torah Ohr." Two other books, "Derech Ha-Chaim" and "Ner Mitzva" were lost during the burning of the Talmud in Padua in 1414. His son Gedaliah is the author of "Shalsheles HaKabbalah". From: https://www.sefaria.org/topics/joseph-ibn-yachya?tab=sources

Atheists challenge monotheism today, especially those who say they belong to a monotheistic religion but worship idolatrous gods. This is a theme that has been found in several Psalms. The god of materialism is a false god. Its followers are more concerned about their wealth and power, shrugging off any consequences of their actions.

In Christianity, there is a ritual called the "deathbed conversion." A sinner or one who committed idolatry with materialism on their deathbed prays that the LORD will forgive them. A pastor or priest arrives and baptizes the person. Everyone present is glad that the baptism ritual was performed. However, did it make a difference? Anyone on their deathbed can say that they believe in Jesus Christ as their savior at the very end.

Issachar reminds us that one must study the Torah and Prophets as a part of their life. This means to live by the Word of the LORD. The last-minute confessions are invalid in the eyes of the LORD. Each human will answer for sin. The Zohar says that the LORD gives people ample time to repent and to make restitution for all sins. If death comes before the sins are repented, that is the person's fault. A last-minute effort to be "saved" will not happen.

Psalm 97

New American Standard 1995	Hebrew

Psa. 97:1 *The LORD ¹reigns, let the ᵇearth rejoice;

Let the many ²ᶜislands be glad.

2　ᵃClouds and thick darkness surround Him;

ᵇRighteousness and justice are the foundation of His throne.

3　ᵃFire goes before Him

And ᵇburns up His adversaries round about.

4　His ᵃlightnings lit up the world;

The earth saw and ᵇtrembled.

5　The mountains ᵃmelted like wax at the presence of the LORD,

At the presence of the ᵇLord of the whole earth.

6　The ᵃheavens declare His righteousness,

And ᵇall the peoples have seen His glory.

Psa. 97:7　Let all those be ashamed who serve ᵃgraven images,

Who boast themselves of ᵇidols;

¹Worship Him, all you ²gods.

8　Zion ¹heard *this* and ᵃwas glad,

And the daughters of Judah have rejoiced

Because of Your judgments, O LORD.

9　For You are the LORD ᵃMost High over all the earth;

You are exalted far ᵇabove all ¹gods.

יְהוָה מָלָךְ תָּגֵל הָאָרֶץ **Psa. 97:1**

יִשְׂמְחוּ אִיִּים רַבִּים ׃ ² עָנָן וַעֲרָפֶל

סְבִיבָיו צֶדֶק וּמִשְׁפָּט מְכוֹן כִּסְאוֹ ׃

³ אֵשׁ לְפָנָיו תֵּלֵךְ וּתְלַהֵט סָבִיב

צָרָיו ׃ ⁴ הֵאִירוּ בְרָקָיו תֵּבֵל רָאֲתָה

וַתָּחֵל הָאָרֶץ ׃ ⁵ הָרִים כַּדּוֹנַג נָמַסּוּ

מִלִּפְנֵי יְהוָה מִלִּפְנֵי אֲדוֹן כָּל־

הָאָרֶץ ׃ ⁶ הִגִּידוּ הַשָּׁמַיִם צִדְקוֹ

וְרָאוּ כָל־הָעַמִּים כְּבוֹדוֹ ׃ ⁷ יֵבֹשׁוּ ׀

כָּל־עֹבְדֵי פֶסֶל הַמִּתְהַלְלִים

בָּאֱלִילִים הִשְׁתַּחֲווּ־לוֹ כָּל־

אֱלֹהִים ׃ ⁸ שָׁמְעָה וַתִּשְׂמַח ׀ צִיּוֹן

וַתָּגֵלְנָה בְּנוֹת יְהוּדָה לְמַעַן

מִשְׁפָּטֶיךָ יְהוָה ׃ ⁹ כִּי־אַתָּה יְהוָה

עֶלְיוֹן עַל־כָּל־הָאָרֶץ מְאֹד נַעֲלֵיתָ

עַל־כָּל־אֱלֹהִים ׃ ¹⁰ אֹהֲבֵי יְהוָה

שִׂנְאוּ רָע שֹׁמֵר נַפְשׁוֹת חֲסִידָיו מִיַּד

רְשָׁעִים יַצִּילֵם ׃ ¹¹ אוֹר זָרֻעַ לַצַּדִּיק

וּלְיִשְׁרֵי־לֵב שִׂמְחָה ׃ ¹² שִׂמְחוּ

צַדִּיקִים בַּיהוָה וְהוֹדוּ לְזֵכֶר

קָדְשׁוֹ ׃

Psa. 97:10 [a]Hate evil, you who love the LORD, Who [b]preserves the souls of His godly ones; He [c]delivers them from the hand of the wicked. 11 [a]Light is sown *like seed* for the righteous And [b]gladness for the upright in heart. 12 Be [a]glad in the LORD, you righteous ones, And [b]give thanks [1]to His holy name.	

References

Psalm 97:1
[1]Or *has assumed Kingship*
[2]Or *coastlands*
[a]Ps 96:10
[b]Ps 96:11
[c]Is 42:10, 12

Psalm 97:2
[a]Ex 19:9; Deut 4:11; 1 Kin 8:12; Ps 18:11
[b]Ps 89:14

Psalm 97:3
[a]Ps 18:8; 50:3; Dan 7:10; Hab 3:5
[b]Mal 4:1; Heb 12:29

Psalm 97:4
[a]Ex 19:16; Ps 77:18
[b]Ps 96:9; 104:32

Psalm 97:5
[a]Ps 46:6; Amos 9:5; Mic 1:4; Nah 1:5
[b]Josh 3:11

Psalm 97:6
[a]Ps 19:1; 50:6
[b]Ps 98:2; Is 6:3; 40:5; 66:18

Psalm 97:7
[1]Or *All the gods have worshiped Him*
[2]Or *supernatural powers*
[a]Ps 78:58; Is 42:17; 44:9, 11; Jer 10:14
[b]Ps 106:36; Jer 50:2; Hab 2:18
[c]Heb 1:6

Psalm 97:8
[1]Or possibly *hears and is glad*
[a]Ps 48:11; Zeph 3:14

Psalm 97:9
[1]Or *supernatural powers*
[a]Ps 83:18
[b]Ex 18:11; Ps 95:3; 96:4; 135:5

Psalm 97:10
[a]Ps 34:14; Prov 8:13; Amos 5:15; Rom 12:9
[b]Ps 31:23; 145:20; Prov 2:8
[c]Ps 37:40; Jer 15:21; Dan 3:28

Psalm 97:11
[a]Job 22:28; Ps 112:4; Prov 4:18
[b]Ps 64:10

Psalm 97:12
[1]Lit *for the memory of His holiness*
[a]Ps 32:11
[b]Ps 30:4

Targum

Psa. 97:1 The LORD reigns, let the earth rejoice, let the many isles be glad. [2] Clouds of glory and darkness are around him; righteousness and justice are the place where his throne is set. [3] Fire will go before him, and it burns around his oppressors. [4] His lightnings illuminate the world; the earth saw and trembled. [5] The mountains will melt like wax in the presence of the LORD, in the presence of the master of all the earth. [6] The angels of the height will tell of his righteousness, and all the peoples will see his glory. [7] All who worship idols will be ashamed, who pride themselves on a false god; and all the peoples who worship a false god will bow down in his presence. [8] The assembly of Zion has heard and rejoiced, and the daughters of the house of Judah exult, because of your judgments, O LORD. [9] For you are the LORD, the supreme one over all the inhabitants of the earth; you are greatly exalted over all that is revered. [10] O you who love the LORD, hate evil, because the Almighty protects the souls of his pious ones; from the hands of the wicked he will deliver them. [11] Light has shone and is hidden for the righteous, and joy for the upright of heart. [12] Be glad, O righteous, in the word of the LORD, and give thanks at the mention of his holy name.

Spiritual Awareness

Introduction

This Psalm was written by Moses and dedicated to the tribe of Joseph (Ephraim and Manassah). Joshua was from the tribe of Joseph and led Israel into the Promised Land and conquered it. The Psalm alludes to the future times of peace.

Verse four

It was a dark era for Israel while they traveled in the wilderness for forty years. The LORD promised to bring the dark era to an end like a thunderstorm. When Joshua took an army to Jericho and walked around the city seven times, the sound of the walls crashing down had to be tremendous. The LORD's people were victorious as they entered the and promised to them through Abraham.

But once His bolts of lightning have lit up the world of man, when the earth has gained insight and gone into labor.

Verses eight and nine

One day the LORD will be worshiped throughout the earth. When this happens, joy will return to Zion, the ancient eternal Sanctuary of the LORD (Jerusalem was where both Temples were built for the LORD. All of Judah will rejoice that day.

But Zion has heard it and is glad, then the daughters of Judah will rejoice because of Your judgments, O LORD;

That you, LORD, are now most high over all the earth, exalted far above all gods. =

Psalm 98

New American Standard 1995	Hebrew
Psa. 98:0 A Psalm. **Psa. 98:1** O sing to the LORD a [a]new song, For He has done [b]wonderful things, His [c]right hand and His [d]holy arm have [1]gained the victory for Him. [2] [a]The LORD has made known His salvation; He has [b]revealed His [1]righteousness in the sight of the nations. [3] He has [a]remembered His lovingkindness and His faithfulness to the house of Israel; [b]All the ends of the earth have seen the salvation of our God. **Psa. 98:4** [a]Shout joyfully to the LORD, all the earth; [b]Break forth and sing for joy and sing praises. [5] Sing praises to the LORD with the [a]lyre, With the lyre and the [1b]sound of melody. [6] With [a]trumpets and the sound of the horn [b]Shout joyfully before [c]the King, the LORD. **Psa. 98:7** Let the [a]sea roar and [1]all it contains, The [b]world and those who dwell in it.	מִזְמוֹר שִׁירוּ לַיהוָה ׀ שִׁיר **Psa. 98:1** חָדָשׁ כִּי־נִפְלָאוֹת עָשָׂה הוֹשִׁיעָה־ לּוֹ יְמִינוֹ וּזְרוֹעַ קָדְשׁוֹ׃ 2 הוֹדִיעַ יְהוָה יְשׁוּעָתוֹ לְעֵינֵי הַגּוֹיִם גִּלָּה צִדְקָתוֹ׃ 3 זָכַר חַסְדּוֹ ׀ וֶאֱמוּנָתוֹ לְבֵית יִשְׂרָאֵל רָאוּ כָל־אַפְסֵי־אָרֶץ אֵת יְשׁוּעַת אֱלֹהֵינוּ׃ 4 הָרִיעוּ לַיהוָה כָּל־הָאָרֶץ פִּצְחוּ וְרַנְּנוּ וְזַמֵּרוּ׃ 5 זַמְּרוּ לַיהוָה בְּכִנּוֹר בְּכִנּוֹר וְקוֹל זִמְרָה׃ 6 בַּחֲצֹצְרוֹת וְקוֹל שׁוֹפָר הָרִיעוּ לִפְנֵי ׀ הַמֶּלֶךְ יְהוָה׃ 7 יִרְעַם הַיָּם וּמְלֹאוֹ תֵּבֵל וְיֹשְׁבֵי בָהּ׃ 8 נְהָרוֹת יִמְחֲאוּ־כָף יַחַד הָרִים יְרַנֵּנוּ׃ 9 לִפְנֵי־יְהוָה כִּי בָא לִשְׁפֹּט הָאָרֶץ יִשְׁפֹּט־תֵּבֵל בְּצֶדֶק וְעַמִּים בְּמֵישָׁרִים׃

<table>
<tr><td>

8   Let the [a]rivers clap their hands,

Let the [b]mountains sing together for joy

9   Before the LORD, for He is coming to [a]judge the earth;

He will judge the world with righteousness

And [b]the peoples with [1]equity.

</td><td>

</td></tr>
</table>

References

Psalm 98:1
[1]Or *accomplished salvation*
[a]Ps 33:3
[b]Ps 40:5; 96:3
[c]Ex 15:6
[d]Is 52:10

Psalm 98:2
[1]I.e. faithfulness to His gracious promises
[a]Is 52:10
[b]Is 62:2; Rom 3:25

Psalm 98:3
[a]Luke 1:54, 72
[b]Ps 22:27

Psalm 98:4
[a]Ps 100:1
[b]Is 44:23

Psalm 98:5
[1]Or *voice of song* (accompanied by music)
[a]Ps 92:3
[b]Is 51:3

Psalm 98:6
[a]Num 10:10; 2 Chr 15:14
[b]Ps 66:1
[c]Ps 47:7

Psalm 98:7
[1]Lit *its fullness*
[a]Ps 96:11
[b]Ps 24:1

Psalm 98:8
[a]Ps 93:3; Is 55:12
[b]Ps 65:12; 89:12

Psalm 98:9
[1]Or *uprightness*
[a]Ps 96:13
[b]Ps 96:10

Targum

Psa. 98:1 A psalm and prophecy. Sing before the LORD a new hymn, for he has done wonders; his right hand has brought redemption, and the arm of his holy presence. ² The LORD has made known his redemption; in the sight of the Gentiles he has revealed his righteousness. ³ He has called to mind his goodness and his truth to the house of Israel, and all the ends of the earth have seen the redemption of our God. ⁴ Give voice in the presence of the LORD, all inhabitants of the earth; rejoice and give praise and make music. ⁵ Sing in the presence of the LORD with harps, with harps and the sound of musical instruments. ⁶ With trumpets and the sound of the horn, give voice in the presence of the king, the LORD. ⁷ Let the sea call out, and its fullness; the world and all who dwell upon it. ⁸ Let the rivers smite their palms; as one, let the mountains sing aloud – ⁹ In the presence of the LORD, for he has come to judge the earth; he will judge the world in righteousness, and the peoples with integrity.

Spiritual Awareness

Introduction

This Psalm was composed by Moses and dedicated to the tribe of Naftali (Deuteronomy 33:23). The love for the LORD that Naftali showed describes the universal abundance and peace which will envelop the earth in the Messianic era. Israel will merit exceptional tranquility and peace of mind, which will prompt them to sing to the LORD.

Notes on this Psalm

This Psalm speaks about the upcoming messianic age. Verses seven to nine describe allegorically what will happen upon the earth. The people who have sinned and not repented will discover their time is up. The LORD will sweep them from the world like a sea roaring toward shore. The earth will rejoice because of what is to come in this era. It is not a love for destruction but rather a rebuilding of all of humanity's world based on the guarantee of growth leading to lasting salvation. When the wicked are removed from the earth, the humans remaining will discover it is easier to serve the LORD. They will never receive any hindrance to doing what the LORD expects all humans to do, that is, to follow the ways of the Torah.

Psalm 99

New American Standard 1995	Hebrew

Psa. 99:1 ^aThe LORD reigns, let the peoples tremble;

He ^{1b}is enthroned *above* the cherubim, let the earth shake!

2 The LORD ¹is ^agreat in Zion,

And He is ^bexalted above all the peoples.

3 Let them praise Your ^agreat and awesome name;

^bHoly is ¹He.

4 The ¹strength of the King ^aloves ²justice;

You have established ^{3b}equity;

You have ^cexecuted ²justice and righteousness in Jacob.

5 ^{1a}Exalt the LORD our God

And ^bworship at His footstool;

^cHoly is He.

Psa. 99:6 ^aMoses and Aaron were among His ^bpriests,

And ^aSamuel was among those who ^ccalled on His name;

They ^dcalled upon the LORD and He answered them.

7 He ^aspoke to them in the pillar of cloud;

They ^bkept His testimonies

And the statute that He gave them.

8 O LORD our God, You ^aanswered them;

You were a ^bforgiving God to them,

יְהוָה מָלָךְ יִרְגְּזוּ עַמִּים יֹשֵׁב Psa. 99:1

כְּרוּבִים תָּנוּט הָאָרֶץ ׃ יְהוָה ²

בְּצִיּוֹן גָּדוֹל וְרָם הוּא עַל־כָּל־

הָעַמִּים ׃ יוֹדוּ שִׁמְךָ גָּדוֹל וְנוֹרָא ³

קָדוֹשׁ הוּא ׃ וְעֹז מֶלֶךְ מִשְׁפָּט ⁴

אָהֵב אַתָּה כּוֹנַנְתָּ מֵישָׁרִים מִשְׁפָּט

וּצְדָקָה בְּיַעֲקֹב אַתָּה עָשִׂיתָ ׃ ⁵

רוֹמְמוּ יְהוָה אֱלֹהֵינוּ וְהִשְׁתַּחֲווּ

לַהֲדֹם רַגְלָיו קָדוֹשׁ הוּא ׃ מֹשֶׁה ⁶

וְאַהֲרֹן בְּכֹהֲנָיו וּשְׁמוּאֵל בְּקֹרְאֵי

שְׁמוֹ קֹרָאִים אֶל־יְהוָה וְהוּא יַעֲנֵם ׃

בְּעַמּוּד עָנָן יְדַבֵּר אֲלֵיהֶם שָׁמְרוּ ⁷

עֵדֹתָיו וְחֹק נָתַן־לָמוֹ ׃ יְהוָה ⁸

אֱלֹהֵינוּ אַתָּה עֲנִיתָם אֵל נֹשֵׂא הָיִיתָ

לָהֶם וְנֹקֵם עַל־עֲלִילוֹתָם ׃ רוֹמְמוּ ⁹

יְהוָה אֱלֹהֵינוּ וְהִשְׁתַּחֲווּ לְהַר קָדְשׁוֹ

כִּי־קָדוֹשׁ יְהוָה אֱלֹהֵינוּ ׃

<table>
<tr><td>

And *yet* an ʿavenger of their *evil* deeds.

⁹ Exalt the LORD our God
And worship at His holy hill,
For holy is the LORD our God.

</td><td></td></tr>
</table>

References

Psalm 99:1
[1]Lit *sits*
[a]Ps 97:1
[b]Ex 25:22; 1 Sam 4:4; Ps 80:1

Psalm 99:2
[1]Or *in Zion is great*
[a]Ps 48:1; Is 12:6
[b]Ps 97:9; 113:4

Psalm 99:3
[1]Or *it*
[a]Deut 28:58; Ps 76:1
[b]Lev 19:2; Josh 24:19; 1 Sam 2:2; Ps 22:3; Is 6:3

Psalm 99:4
[1]Or *You have established in equity the strength of the King who loves justice*
[2]Or *judgment*
[3]Or *uprightness*
[a]Ps 11:7; 33:5
[b]Ps 17:2; 98:9
[c]Ps 103:6; 146:7; Jer 23:5

Psalm 99:5
[1]The verb is plural
[a]Ps 34:3; 107:32; 118:28
[b]Ps 132:7
[c]Ps 99:3

Psalm 99:6
[a]Jer 15:1
[b]Ex 24:6-8; 29:26; 40:23-27; Lev 8:1-30
[c]1 Sam 7:9; 12:18; Ps 22:4, 5
[d]Ex 15:25; 32:30-34

Psalm 99:7
[a]Ex 33:9; Num 12:5
[b]Ps 105:28

Psalm 99:8
[a]Ps 106:44
[b]Num 14:20; Ps 78:38
[c]Ex 32:28; Num 20:12; Ps 95:11; 107:12

Targum

Psa. 99:1 The LORD reigns, the peoples will tremble; he whose presence abides among the cherubim will shake the earth. ² The LORD is great in Zion; and he is high over all the Gentiles. ³ They will confess his name, great and fearful; he is holy. ⁴ And you love the strength of the king of justice; you have established integrity; you have made justice and righteousness in Jacob. ⁵ Sing praise in the presence of the LORD our God, and bow down towards his sanctuary; he is holy. ⁶ Moses and Aaron are among his priests who gave their life for the people of the LORD, and Samuel prayed for them before the LORD, like the fathers of old, who prayed in his name; they would pray in his presence and he would answer them. ⁷ In the pillar of glorious clouds he would speak with them; they kept the commandments [of] his testimony, and the covenant that he gave to them. ⁸ O LORD our God, you answered them; you were a forgiving God for your people for their sake, and take vengeance for their deeds. ⁹ Sing praise in the presence of the LORD our God, and bow down towards the mount of his sanctuary, for the LORD our God is holy.

Spiritual Awareness

Introduction

This Psalm was composed by Moses and dedicated to the tribe of Dan. Dan was a strong tribe, and Moses said that Dan would have the opportunity to conquer the nations that were not obeying the LORD's Law. When the day of judgment comes, there will be a war against Gog and Magog. Israel will win the war, and the LORD's universal power will become unchallenged. Where are Gog and Magog located? Errico Rocco (Aramaic scholar) believes that Gog and Magog refer to Mongolia and China.

Verse one

During the days of the Temples in Jerusalem, the people believed that the LORD sat upon the cherubim that sat on the top of the Ark of the Covenant. It was the Shekinah that sat on the Ark. The book of Ezekiel describes what Shekinah appeared as when she left the Temple because the Babylonians were about to destroy the Temple. The Shekinah did not want to leave but was forced to leave.

God has begun His reign; the nations tremble. He has established Himself upon the Cherubim; the earth gives way.

Notes about the Psalm

When the Messianic period commences, the Messiah will come to earth. The Zohar (the mystic writings) speaks about two Messiahs, Messiah ben Joseph and Messiah ben David. This idea arises from Zecharaiah 9:9, which says that the Messiah will be found riding a donkey and colt. The spiritual awareness is that the first Messiah,

Messiah ben Joseph, will come to Israel to restore its spirituality. The nation will return to pure worship that is acceptable to the LORD. This first Messiah will return the secret Torah Moses received on Mount Sinai but was lost over the centuries. The spirituality of Israel must be restored before judgment day.

The second Messiah, Messiah ben David, will come afterward. This Messiah will restore the Kingdom of Israel and destroy any nation, not in allegiance with the LORD. The war of Gog and Magog will occur at that time. Therefore, the second Messiah is the warrior Messiah that the Israelites were waiting for when the Romans controlled the land of Judea.

An important note is that nothing in the Zohar indicates that the two Messiahs could not be the same person. Christianity moved toward this idea because the idea of the Messiah coming twice to earth is found in the Mithras cult. Mithras came to raise the spirituality of his followers. Those who followed Mithras were offered salvation through Mithras' death. When Paul converted the Mithras House Churches into Jesus House Churches, the theological doctrine of the Messiah coming twice to earth was retained.

For Jewish people, Jesus is not seen as the Messiah because they thought the Messiah ben David, would come first. This Messiah is the warrior they cried out for. The Christian view of Jesus being the Suffering Servant of Isaiah, chapters 50 to 55, was added to their doctrine because it fit into Jesus' life. These chapters would fit into the life of any prophet from the LORD. The sages said that these Isaiah chapters describe the nation of Israel as the suffering servant. Israel has worshiped and followed the LORD's ways for centuries and has always been under the oppression of foreign nations. Even when David and Solomon reigned, they still had to deal with invasions from surrounding nations.

Anyone who stands up for the LORD and tries to do His Will can find their life turning into the Suffering Servant of Isaiah 50-55. There are many forms of suffering that a person may have to endure if the person wants to fully serve the LORD.

Psalm 100

New American Standard 1995	Hebrew
Psa. 100:0 A Psalm for †Thanksgiving. **Psa. 100:1** ᵃShout joyfully to the LORD, all the earth. 2 ᵃServe the LORD with gladness; ᵇCome before Him with joyful singing. 3 Know that ᵃthe LORD ¹Himself is God; It is He who has ᵇmade us, and ²not we ourselves; *We are* ᶜHis people and the sheep of His pasture. **Psa. 100:4** Enter His gates ᵃwith ¹thanksgiving *And* His courts with praise. Give thanks to Him, ᵇbless His name. 5 For ᵃthe LORD is good; ᵇHis lovingkindness is everlasting And His ᶜfaithfulness to all generations.	**Psa. 100:1** מִזְמ֥וֹר לְתוֹדָ֑ה הָרִ֥יעוּ ² לַֽיהוָ֗ה כָּל־הָאָֽרֶץ׃ עִבְד֣וּ אֶת־ יְהוָ֣ה בְּשִׂמְחָ֑ה בֹּ֥אוּ לְ֝פָנָ֗יו בִּרְנָנָֽה׃ ³ דְּע֗וּ כִּֽי־יְהוָה֮ ה֤וּא אֱלֹ֫הִ֥ים ה֣וּא עָ֭שָׂנוּ וְלֹ֣א [וְלֹ֣ו] אֲנַ֑חְנוּ עַ֝מּ֗וֹ וְצֹ֣אן מַרְעִיתֽוֹ׃ ⁴ בֹּ֤אוּ שְׁעָרָ֨יו ׀ בְּתוֹדָ֗ה חֲצֵרֹתָ֥יו בִּתְהִלָּ֑ה הֽוֹדוּ־ל֝֗וֹ בָּרֲכ֥וּ שְׁמֽוֹ׃ ⁵ כִּי־ט֣וֹב יְ֭הֹוָה לְעוֹלָ֣ם חַסְדּ֑וֹ וְעַד־דֹּ֥ר וָ֝דֹ֗ר אֱמוּנָתֽוֹ׃

References

Psalm 100:0
†Or *thank offering*

Psalm 100:1
*a*Ps 95:1; 98:4, 6

Psalm 100:2
*a*Deut 12:11, 12; 28:47
*b*Ps 95:2

Psalm 100:3
[1]Or *He*
[2]Some mss read *His we are*
*a*Deut 4:35; 1 Kin 18:39; Ps 46:10
*b*Job 10:3, 8; Ps 95:6; 119:73
*c*Ps 74:1, 2; 95:7; Is 40:11; Ezek 34:30, 31

Psalm 100:4
[1]Or *a thank offering*
*a*Ps 95:2; 116:17
*b*Ps 96:2

Psalm 100:5
*a*1 Chr 16:34; 2 Chr 5:13; 7:3; Ezra 3:11; Ps 25:8; 86:5; 106:1; 107:1; 118:1; Jer 33:11; Nah 1:7
*b*Ps 136:1
*c*Ps 119:90

Targum

Psa. 100:1 A psalm on the offering of thanksgiving. Give a shout in the presence of the LORD, all inhabitants of the earth. [2] Worship in the presence of the LORD with joy; come before him with praise. [3] Make it known, for the LORD is God; he has made us and we are his, his people and the flock of his pasture. [4] Enter his gates with thanksgiving, his courts with praise; give thanks in his presence, bless his name. [5] For the LORD is good, his goodness is forever, and his faithfulness lasts for all generations.

Spiritual Awareness

Introduction

This is the last Psalm composed by Moses. It was sung in the Temple during the Thanksgiving offering. This offering was brought to the Temple after having survived a great danger. Not a day in one's life occurs without danger. Most of the time, a person is oblivious to the dangers and that the LORD protects from hazards performing countless miracles of salvation. Therefore, today it is sung every day.

Verse five

The Psalmist calls out to the Sefirah Chesed for the LORD's lovingkindness.

For God is good; the Sefirah Chesed endures forever giving us the LORD's love, and His guiding faithfulness extends to every generation.

APPENDIX

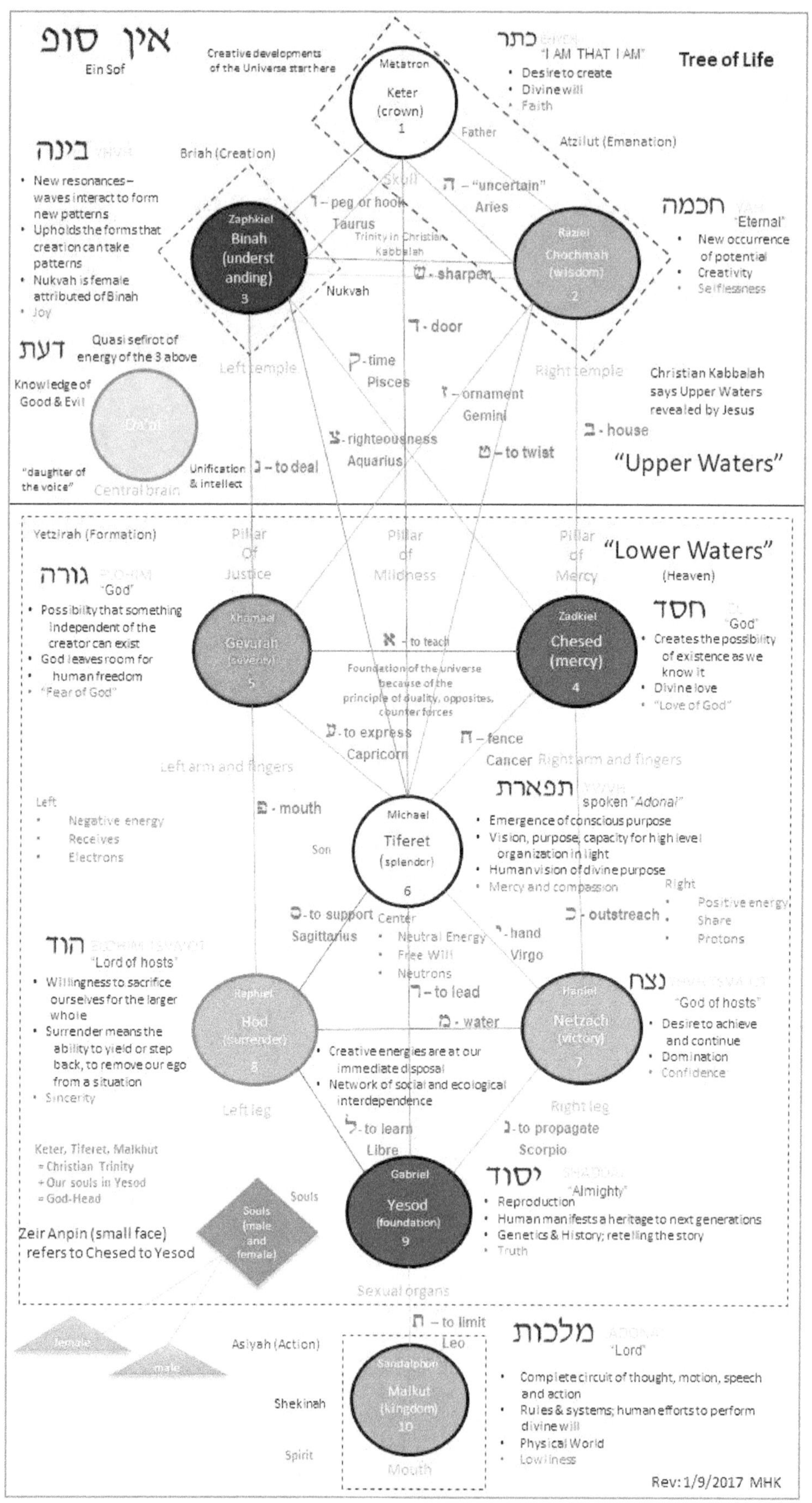
אין סוף
Ein Sof
Tree of Life
Creative developments of the Universe start here
כתר
"I AM THAT I AM"
Desire to create
Divine will
Faith
Metatron
Keter (crown)
1
Father
Atzilut (Emanation)
בינה
New resonances – waves interact to form new patterns
Upholds the forms that creation can take patterns
Nukvah is female attributed of Binah
Joy
Briah (Creation)
Zaphkiel
Binah (understanding)
3
Skull
ו – peg or hook
Taurus
Trinity in Christian Kabbalah
Nukvah
ה – "uncertain"
Aries
ש – sharpen
חכמה
"Eternal"
New occurrence of potential
Creativity
Selflessness
Raziel
Chochmah (wisdom)
2
Right temple
דעת
Quasi sefirot of energy of the 3 above
Knowledge of Good & Evil
Daat
"daughter of the voice"
Central brain
Left temple
ד - door
ק - time
Pisces
ז – ornament
Gemini
צ - righteousness
Aquarius
נ – to deal
Unification & intellect
ת – to twist
ב - house
Christian Kabbalah says Upper Waters revealed by Jesus
"Upper Waters"
Yetzirah (Formation)
Pillar Of Justice
Pillar of Mildness
Pillar of Mercy
"Lower Waters"
(Heaven)
גורה
"God"
Possibility that something independent of the creator can exist
God leaves room for human freedom
"Fear of God"
Khamael
Gevurah (severity)
5
א - to teach
Foundation of the universe because of the principle of duality, opposites, counter forces
Zadkiel
Chesed (mercy)
4
חסד
"God"
Creates the possibility of existence as we know it
Divine love
"Love of God"
ע - to express
Capricorn
ח – fence
Cancer
Right arm and fingers
Left arm and fingers
Left
Negative energy
Receives
Electrons
פ - mouth
Michael
Tiferet (splendor)
6
Son
תפארת
spoken "Adonai"
Emergence of conscious purpose
Vision, purpose, capacity for high level organization in light
Human vision of divine purpose
Mercy and compassion
Right
Positive energy
Share
Protons
ס - to support
Center
Sagittarius
Neutral Energy
Free Will
Neutrons
כ - outstreach
י - hand
Virgo
הוד
"Lord of hosts"
Willingness to sacrifice ourselves for the larger whole
Surrender means the ability to yield or step back, to remove our ego from a situation
Sincerity
Raphiel
Hod (surrender)
8
ר - to lead
מ - water
Haniel
Netzach (victory)
7
נצח
"God of hosts"
Desire to achieve and continue
Domination
Confidence
Left leg
Creative energies are at our immediate disposal
Network of social and ecological interdependence
Right leg
Keter, Tiferet, Malkhut
= Christian Trinity
+ Our souls in Yesod
= God-Head
ל - to learn
Libre
נ - to propagate
Scorpio
Zeir Anpin (small face) refers to Chesed to Yesod
Souls
Gabriel
Yesod (foundation)
9
Souls (male and female)
יסוד
"Almighty"
Reproduction
Human manifests a heritage to next generations
Genetics & History; retelling the story
Truth
Sexual organs
Female
male
ת – to limit
Leo
Asiyah (Action)
Sandalphon
Malkut (kingdom)
10
Shekinah
Spirit
Mouth
מלכות
"Lord"
Complete circuit of thought, motion, speech and action
Rules & systems; human efforts to perform divine will
Physical World
Lowliness
Rev: 1/9/2017 MHK

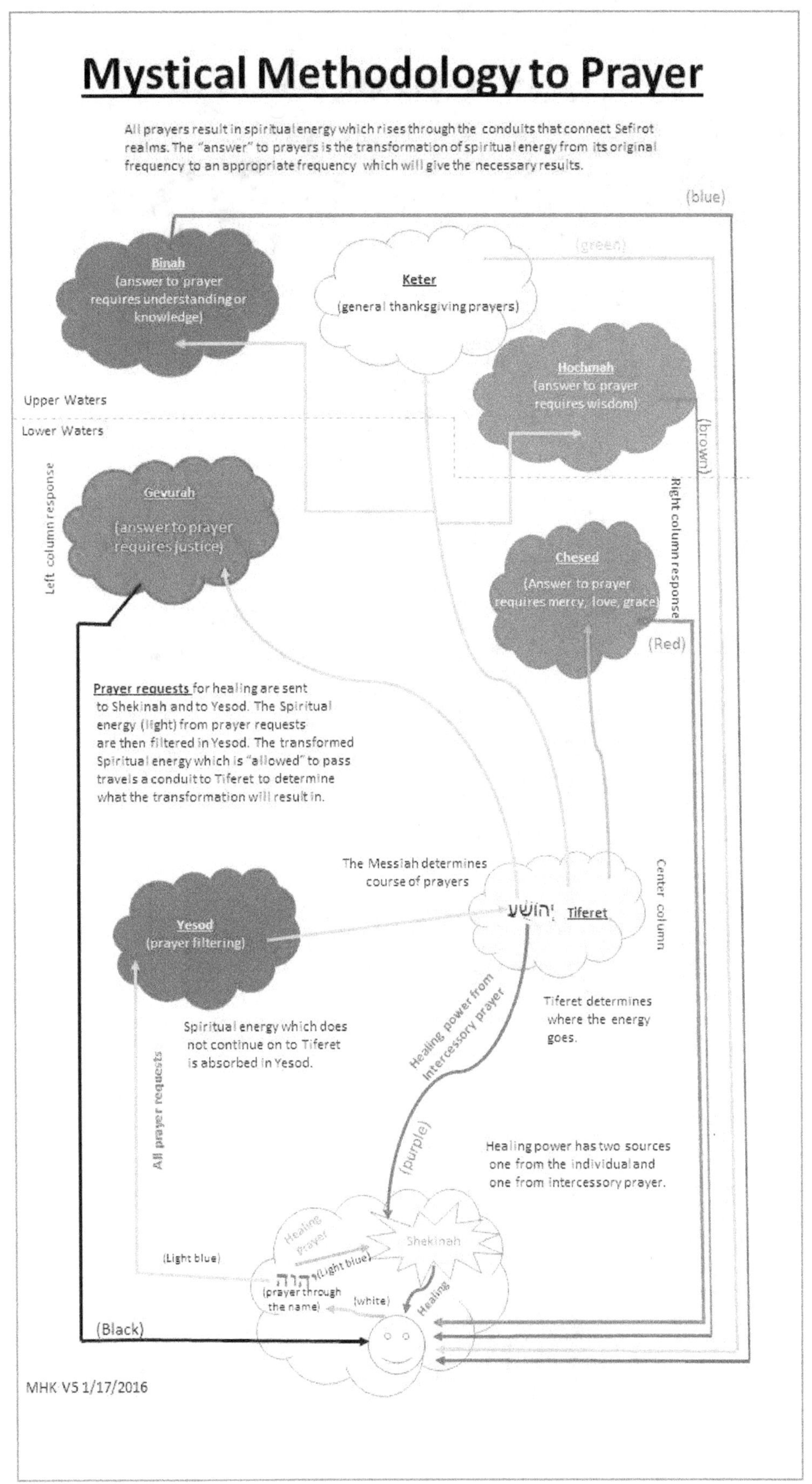

Mystical Methodology to Prayer
All prayers result in spiritual energy which rises through the conduits that connect Sefirot realms. The "answer" to prayers is the transformation of spiritual energy from its original frequency to an appropriate frequency which will give the necessary results.
(blue)
(green)
Binah
(answer to prayer requires understanding or knowledge)
Keter
(general thanksgiving prayers)
Hochmah
(answer to prayer requires wisdom)
Upper Waters
Lower Waters
(brown)
Left column response
Gevurah
(answer to prayer requires justice)
Chesed
(Answer to prayer requires mercy, love, grace)
Right column response
(Red)
Prayer requests for healing are sent to Shekinah and to Yesod. The Spiritual energy (light) from prayer requests are then filtered in Yesod. The transformed Spiritual energy which is "allowed" to pass travels a conduit to Tiferet to determine what the transformation will result in.
The Messiah determines course of prayers
Center column
יהושע Tiferet
Yesod
(prayer filtering)
Tiferet determines where the energy goes.
Healing power from Intercessory prayer
Spiritual energy which does not continue on to Tiferet is absorbed in Yesod.
All prayer requests
(purple)
Healing power has two sources one from the individual and one from intercessory prayer.
Healing prayer
Shekinah
(Light blue)
(Light blue)
יהוה
(prayer through the name)
(white)
Healing
(Black)
MHK V5 1/17/2016

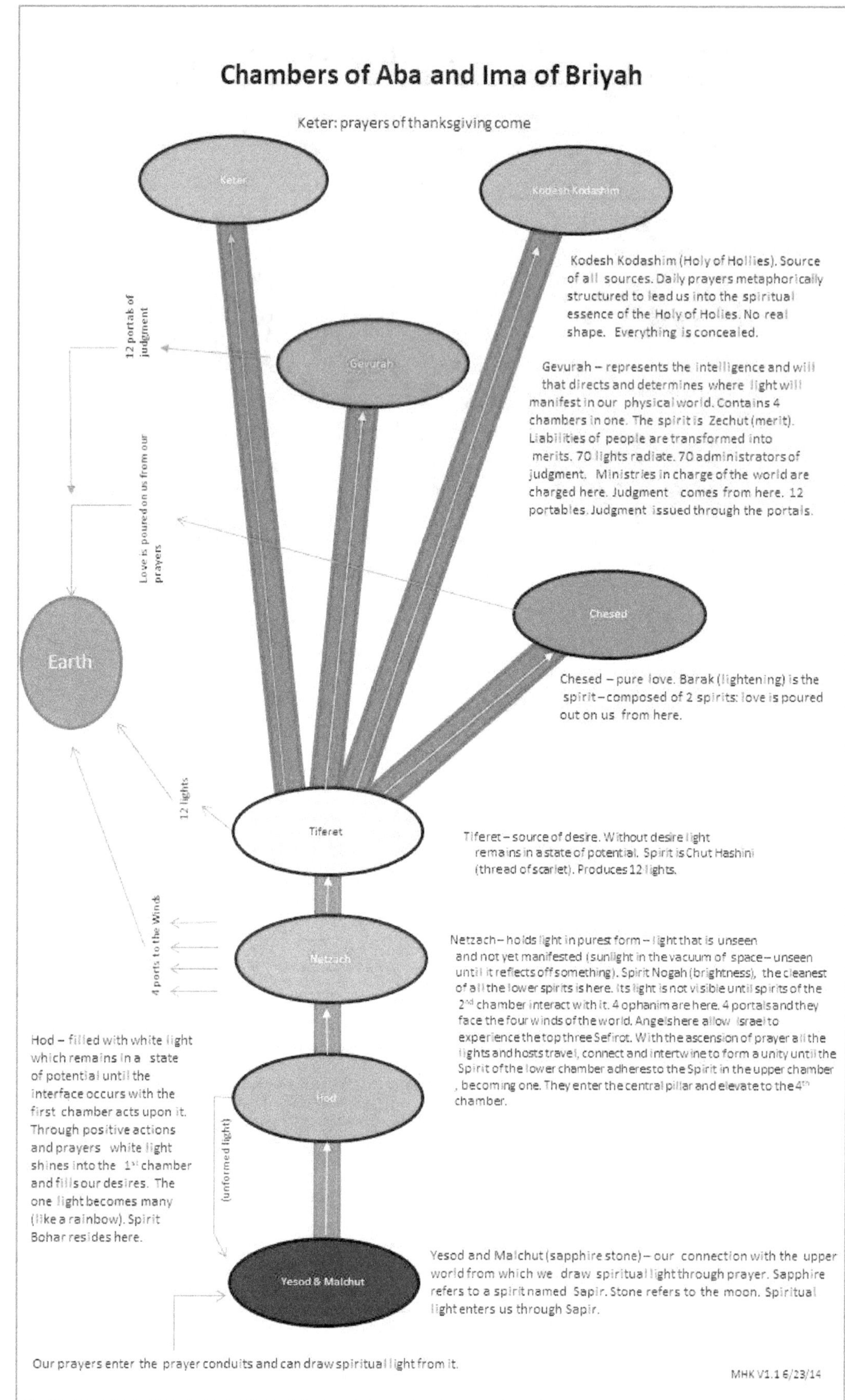

Chambers of Aba and Ima of Briyah
Keter: prayers of thanksgiving come
Keter
Kodesh Kodashim
Gevurah
Chesed
Earth
Tiferet
Netzach
Hod
Yesod & Malchut
12 portals of judgment
Love is poured on us from our prayers
12 lights
4 ports to the Winds
(unformed light)
Kodesh Kodashim (Holy of Hollies). Source of all sources. Daily prayers metaphorically structured to lead us into the spiritual essence of the Holy of Holies. No real shape. Everything is concealed.
Gevurah – represents the intelligence and will that directs and determines where light will manifest in our physical world. Contains 4 chambers in one. The spirit is Zechut (merit). Liabilities of people are transformed into merits. 70 lights radiate. 70 administrators of judgment. Ministries in charge of the world are charged here. Judgment comes from here. 12 portables. Judgment issued through the portals.
Chesed – pure love. Barak (lightening) is the spirit – composed of 2 spirits: love is poured out on us from here.
Tiferet – source of desire. Without desire light remains in a state of potential. Spirit is Chut Hashini (thread of scarlet). Produces 12 lights.
Netzach – holds light in purest form – light that is unseen and not yet manifested (sunlight in the vacuum of space – unseen until it reflects off something). Spirit Nogah (brightness), the cleanest of all the lower spirits is here. Its light is not visible until spirits of the 2nd chamber interact with it. 4 ophanim are here. 4 portals and they face the four winds of the world. Angels here allow Israel to experience the top three Sefirot. With the ascension of prayer all the lights and hosts travel, connect and intertwine to form a unity until the Spirit of the lower chamber adheres to the Spirit in the upper chamber, becoming one. They enter the central pillar and elevate to the 4th chamber.
Hod – filled with white light which remains in a state of potential until the interface occurs with the first chamber acts upon it. Through positive actions and prayers white light shines into the 1st chamber and fills our desires. The one light becomes many (like a rainbow). Spirit Bohar resides here.
Yesod and Malchut (sapphire stone) – our connection with the upper world from which we draw spiritual light through prayer. Sapphire refers to a spirit named Sapir. Stone refers to the moon. Spiritual light enters us through Sapir.
Our prayers enter the prayer conduits and can draw spiritual light from it.
MHK V1.1 6/23/14

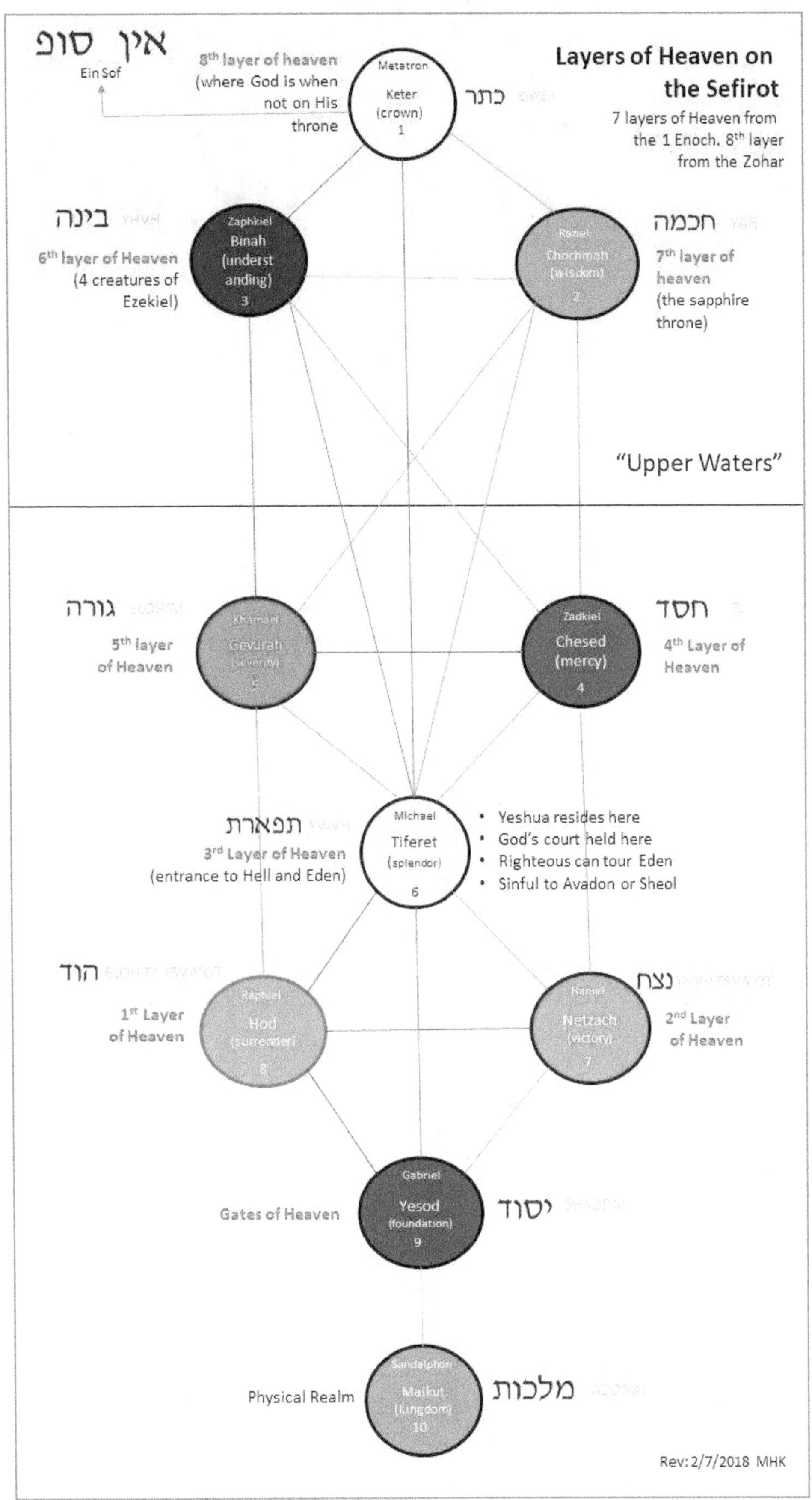

אין סוף
Ein Sof

8th layer of heaven (where God is when not on His throne)

Layers of Heaven on the Sefirot
7 layers of Heaven from the 1 Enoch. 8th layer from the Zohar

Metatron
Keter (crown)
1
כתר

בינה
6th layer of Heaven (4 creatures of Ezekiel)
Zaphkiel
Binah (understanding)
3

חכמה
7th layer of heaven (the sapphire throne)
Raziel
Chochmah (wisdom)
2

"Upper Waters"

גורה
5th layer of Heaven
Khamael
Gevurah (severity)
5

חסד
4th Layer of Heaven
Zadkiel
Chesed (mercy)
4

תפארת
3rd Layer of Heaven (entrance to Hell and Eden)
Michael
Tiferet (splendor)
6

• Yeshua resides here
• God's court held here
• Righteous can tour Eden
• Sinful to Avadon or Sheol

הוד
1st Layer of Heaven
Raphael
Hod (surrender)
8

נצח
2nd Layer of Heaven
Haniel
Netzach (victory)
7

Gates of Heaven
Gabriel
Yesod (foundation)
9
יסוד

Physical Realm
Sandalphon
Malkut (kingdom)
10
מלכות

Rev: 2/7/2018 MHK